THE RICHES OF SIMPLICITY

Selected Writings of
FRANCIS AND CLARE

Upper Room Spiritual Classics — Series 2

Selected, edited, and introduced by
Keith Beasley-Topliffe

UPPER
ROOM BOOKS

The Riches of Simplicity: Selected Writings of Francis and Clare

© 1998 by Upper Room Books. All Rights Reserved.

Upper Room Web address: http://www.upperroom.org

Scripture quotations are from the New Revised Standard Version of the Bible, © 1989 by the Division of Christian Education of the National Council of Churches of Christ in the USA. Used by permission. All rights reserved.

Selections from *Francis and Clare* translation and introduction by Regis J. Armstrong, O.F.M. CAP and Ignatius C. Brady, O.F.M. ©1982 by the Missionary Society of St. Paul the Apostle in the State of New York. Used by permission of Paulist Press.

While every effort has been made to secure permission from the rightful copyright holder, we apologize for any inadvertent oversight or error.

Art direction: Michele Wetherbee
Interior design and layout: Nancy Cole

First Printing: October 1998

Library of Congress Cataloging-in-Publication Data

Francis, of Assisi, Saint, 1182–1226.
    The riches of simplicity : selected writings of Francis and Clare.
        p.   cm. — (Upper Room spiritual classics. Series 2)
    Includes bibliographical references.
    ISBN 0-8358-0834-3
    1. Spiritual life—Catholic Church. 2. Simplicity—Religious aspects—Catholic Church. 3. Poverty—Religious aspects—Catholic Church. 4. Catholic Church—Doctrines. I. Clare, of Assisi, Saint, 1194–1253. II. Title. III. Series.
BX2179.F64E5   1998
271'.3022—dc21   97-33190
                                                        CIP
                                                        r97

TABLE OF CONTENTS

INTRODUCTION

George Bernard Shaw once wrote that Christ "has not been a failure yet, for nobody has ever been sane enough to try his way." He was not quite right, for through the ages there have been a few men and women who have truly tried to live a Christlike life shaped to their own times. Perhaps none have succeeded as well as the two saints of Assisi, Francis and Clare.

Though their writings are few, they burn with a love for God and a devotion to sacrificial living. They gave up literally everything—possessions, family, even their own wills—to follow their beloved, Jesus, who had no place to lay his head.

Because their lives as much as their words have inspired Christians for seven centuries, this volume contains selections from some of the earliest biographies in addition to the writings of Francis and Clare.

THE WORLD OF FRANCIS AND CLARE

The early thirteenth century bore the fruit of the flowering of learning and prosperity begun in the twelfth century. Towns grew into cities throughout Europe, as craftspeople and merchants came together in them. In several of the new cities of Italy, the craft and merchant guilds took over the government from hereditary lords. The middle class grew in numbers and prosperity. Fortunes were made in trade and banking, and the pursuit of wealth often took precedence over the pursuit of holiness.

The church had reached the peak of its power over society. The king of England (John) and the emperor of Germany (Frederick II) traveled to Rome to pay homage to Pope Innocent III, not as their spiritual leader, but as their feudal overlord. At the same time, a spirit of reform swept through the Church, both in the decrees of the Fourth Lateran Council (1215) and in new monastic orders such as the Lesser Brothers (or Friars Minor) begun by Francis and the Order of Preachers begun by Dominic at about the same time.

The twelfth century also produced the epic poems of chivalry and courtly love, many based on stories of King Arthur and his knights. These poems lifted up an ideal of knighthood—boldness, feats of strength, devotion to a noble lady. Francis stood this ideal on its head with his devotion to Lady Poverty.

THE LIVES OF FRANCIS AND CLARE

Francis was the son of Pietro di Bernardone, a wealthy cloth merchant of Assisi, and his French wife, Pica. Pietro was away buying cloth when Pica gave birth to her first child, late in 1181. Pica had the baby baptized as Giovanni or John. When Pietro returned, he insisted the child be called Francesco (Frenchy). As Francis (Francesco) grew, he was trained not only in the cloth trade, but also in song and poetry and the art of war: all the marks of a well-bred (if not noble) young gentleman.

In 1202 Francis went to war. He was captured in his first major battle and spent a year in a dungeon with other prisoners of war. When he returned to Assisi, he prepared to join another army but became ill and had to go home again. During that illness, Francis had time to reevaluate his life. Old amusements no longer offered pleasure. He went off by himself to pray and to do good works, first helping people with leprosy and then restoring old churches near Assisi: San Damiano (which became Clare's convent, San Pietro) and a little church devoted to Mary called the Portiuncula, which became the center of the Franciscan movement. He sold all he owned to pay for the restorations. When he sold some of his father's cloth to raise more money, his father wanted him arrested. In the town square, Francis returned the money and even all of his clothes and accepted an old cloak from the bishop of Assisi as his only clothing. Francis chalked a cross on the cloak and set off to beg for money to continue his church repairs.

Others joined Francis in a revised mission of spreading the gospel. When there were a dozen with him, Francis decided to seek official approval of the group. The "penitents from Assisi" set out for Rome in the Spring of 1209 to present a simple Rule of Life to Pope Innocent III, who received Francis warmly. This early Rule was so filled with references to the Gospels that one cardinal remarked, "If we reject the Rule of this poor man as impractical, don't we at the same time affirm that the gospel is impractical?" The Brothers lived first at Rivo Torto, then at the

Portiuncula, at least when they were not out preaching, working, or begging.

Among the people who came to Francis for guidance was a young woman named Clare. Her parents, Favarone di Offreduccia and his wife, Ortolana, were members of the old nobility of Assisi. Clare's mother had made pilgrimages to Rome and the Holy Land. A vision before her first daughter's birth (about 1193) convinced her that the child would be a light for many souls, and so she was named Chiara, or "brilliant." Clare (Chiara) was taught to read and write in Latin. She supported the repair projects of Francis with her own money, and at age eighteen (in 1212) she ran away from home to join him. Since having a young woman among the Brothers was unthinkable, Francis housed Clare and a few companions with Benedictine nuns. When her fifteen-year-old sister, Agnes, followed her, Clare's family protested to the bishop, who nevertheless recognized their religious professions as valid and gave them San Damiano to be their convent, the first home of the Order of Poor Ladies or Poor Clares. There they followed a simple Rule given to them by Francis.

Others came to Francis and Clare who could not "leave the world" to become Brothers or Poor Ladies but still wanted to follow their guidance. For them Francis created a Third Order, a way of life calling for simple living, devotion to the sacraments, a daily pattern of prayer, and fellowship with other "tertiaries."

But Francis did not want to be an administrator. So, in 1217, the order was divided into regional "provinces," each led by a Minister Provincial. Francis appointed Brother Elias to be Minister General over the whole order. He wanted to be free to preach, especially to Muslims. Yet he meant to be a crusader with words, not arms.

Twice, however, Francis's "crusade" was foiled: by storms at sea in 1212 and by illness in 1215. The third time, in 1219, he arrived at Damietta in Egypt, where crusaders were besieging a Saracen army. Francis walked through the lines and spoke to the sultan, who listened politely, but then sent him home.

By 1220, there were about ten thousand Brothers and thus they needed a more formal structure. The simple Rule informally approved by Innocent III was expanded and formalized in 1221. After further revision, the new Rule was approved by Honorius III on November 23, 1223.

Once, at Christmas 1223, Francis preached at the church in Greccio. He set up a manger in the church and led in an ox and an ass as he told about the birth of Christ in a stable. Modern love for the manger scene, from small carvings to living pageants, goes back to this moment.

By 1223 Francis was worn out by his travels and he could no longer do manual work. He spent much of his time in prayer, often in mountain caves. In 1224, he went to La Verna, a mountain plateau a hundred miles north of Assisi. There, on September

14, while Francis prayed to experience fully both Christ's passion and his love for God, he saw a vision of Christ both crucified and glorious. From that time on, Francis had sores in his hands, feet, and side corresponding to the wounds of Christ, the "stigmata." Though Francis tried to keep the wounds covered with bandages, several of his closest friends saw them and later testified about them.

After further illness and partial blindness, Francis returned home to the Portiuncula to die. Clare and her sisters took care of him during his last days. He was just forty-five when he died on October 3, 1226. Francis was officially declared a saint two years later by Pope Gregory IX.

Clare lived for another twenty-seven years after the death of Francis. During that time she struggled to maintain the ideal of poverty against well-meaning offers from bishops who wanted to make her life a little easier. The bishops who were appointed as protectors of her order wrote a series of Rules for the Poor Ladies based on the Benedictine Rule. Finally, in 1252, Clare wrote her own Rule, which was approved by Pope Innocent IV at Assisi on August 9, 1253. The official copy, signed by Innocent, was taken to Clare immediately. She died two days later and, like Francis, was proclaimed a saint two years later.

FURTHER READING

Many editions of the writings of Francis have been published. Clare's writings are less widely available, however. *Francis and Clare: The Complete Works* (Paulist Press) contains all the known writings of both.

There have been many biographies of Francis and Clare, the earliest written within a few years of their deaths. The most popular collection of stories about Francis is *The Little Flowers*, available in several modern translations. One of the best modern biographies is *Saint Francis of Assisi: A Biography* by Omer Englebert. Nikos Kazantzakis and Murray Bodo have written imaginative modern retellings of the stories of Francis and Clare.

NOTE ON THE TEXT

The following selections have been taken from a variety of sources. Older translations have been modernized. Selections have been edited for length and inclusive language. Where possible, scriptural references have been conformed to the language of the New Revised Standard Version (indicated by *italics*).

FRANCIS BEGINS TO SERVE GOD

From *The Second Life of Saint Francis*, Chapters 5 to 7

Thomas of Celano joined Francis' order about 1215 and was selected by Pope Gregory IX to write a brief account of the life and miracles of Francis on the occasion of his canonization in 1228. About sixteen years later the Minister General of the order, Crescentius, asked him to write an expanded version with more emphasis on the inner life and spiritual experiences of the saint. He did this in consultation with three of the earliest Brothers: Leo, Angelo, and Rufino. This selection concerns Francis's encounter with a person who had leprosy and the break with his family. As it begins, Francis has begun to spend time in prayer and to wear a hair shirt under his everyday clothes for penance.

Already he wore the spirit of religion underneath his worldly attire, and withdrawing from frequented places to solitary ones, he was often admonished by visitations of the Holy Spirit. He was carried away and drawn on by the great sweetness that was shed upon him so abundantly even from the first that it never left him as long as he lived. But while he was frequenting out-of-the-way places that were suitable for prayer, the devil strove to disturb his devotions by evil visions. The devil made him think of a woman of his city who was monstrously hunchbacked and threatened to make him resemble her if he did not give up what he had begun. But the Lord of salvation and grace encouraged him.

"Francis," said God to him in the Spirit, "you will exchange what you have loved carnally and vainly for spiritual things. If you want to follow me, take the bitter instead of the sweet and despise yourself, for you will find the taste of the things I speak about reversed." Immediately he was compelled to obey the divine urging and was led to actual experience.

Now among all the wretched spectacles of the world Francis naturally shrank from people with leprosy. But one day while he was riding near Assisi he met a leper, and though the leper made him feel disgust and horror, still, rather than transgress the commandment and break the obligation of his pledged faith, he dismounted and rushed over to the leper to kiss him. When the leper held out his hand as though to receive something, he received money and a kiss with it. Francis immediately remounted, and as he looked around this way and that, though the country was open on all sides and there were no obstacles, he could not see that leper at all. Then he was filled with wonder and joy. He went where the lepers lived, and as he gave each one money, Francis kissed him on the hand and mouth. Thus he took the bitter instead of the sweet and bravely prepared to perform the rest.

Being perfectly changed in heart (and soon to be changed in body too), he was walking one day by the church of San Damiano, which was in ruins and forsaken by all. Led by the Spirit, he went in to pray. He fell down before the crucifix in devout supplication. While he was thus moved, at once—a thing unheard of for ages—the painted image of Christ crucified moved its lips and addressed him by name. "Francis," it said, "repair my house, which as you see is falling into ruin." Francis, trembling and in no small amazement, nearly became deranged by this address. He prepared to obey and was intent on fulfilling the commandment. But since he felt that the change he had undergone was inexplicable, we should be silent concerning what he could not express. From that time, compassion for the Crucified was fixed in his holy soul, and (as we may suppose) the stigmata of the Passion were deeply imprinted on his heart though not as yet on his flesh. It was a wondrous thing! Who is not amazed by it? Who ever heard the like? Who doubts that Francis now returning to his native land appeared crucified when, though he had not altogether set aside the world outwardly, Christ by a new and unheard of miracle spoke to him from the wood of the cross? From that hour, therefore, when the Beloved spoke to him, his soul was melted, and soon the love of the heart appeared by the wounds of the body. After that he could not refrain from weeping, even crying out loud, whenever he saw the passion of Christ depicted. He filled the air with groans and would not be comforted as he remembered the wounds of Christ. He met an intimate friend, to whom he disclosed the cause of his grief, and at once his friend was moved to tears of sorrow.

But he did not forget that holy image, nor did he in any way neglect its bidding. Immediately he gave money to a priest that he might buy a lamp and oil, so that the sacred image would not be deprived, even for a moment, of its due honor of light. Then he diligently hurried to accomplish the rest and worked untiringly on the repair of that church. Although the divine words addressed to him referred to the church that Christ acquired by his own blood, Francis would not reach this highest understanding at once. He had to pass gradually from the flesh to the spirit.

Now that Francis was applying himself to works of piety, his father, Pietro, persecuted him. He considered Christ's service madness and assailed his son with curses. So God's servant called to his aid a certain lowborn and very simple man whom he adopted in place of his father, asking him to bless him whenever his father redoubled his curses. Truly Francis turned the prophet's word into action and showed by deeds what that saying means, "Let them curse, but you will bless."

At the persuasion of the bishop of the city, a very pious man, who told him that he might not spend anything ill-gotten on sacred purposes, Francis gave up to his father some money he had meant to devote to the work at the church. In the hearing of the many who had gathered he cried, "Henceforth I may freely say 'our Father in heaven,' not any more Father Pietro di Bernardone. Look, I not only restore the money to him but also give up all my clothes. Naked therefore will I go to the Lord." O liberal spirit of the man to whom now Christ alone is sufficient! It was then found that the man of God had been wearing sackcloth under his clothes, rejoicing more in the reality than in the appearance of virtue.

 # PRAYER AND PREACHING

More than a century after the death of Francis, legends about the saint and his companions were collected from a variety of sources. One of these sources spoke of the individual stories as "flowers gathered from a pleasant meadow," and so the collection came to be called The Little Flowers. *One of the most famous stories is about Francis preaching to birds.*

Shortly after his conversion, the humble servant of Christ, Saint Francis, having already gathered many companions and received them into the order, was anxious and doubtful about what he should do. Should he devote himself wholly to prayer or sometimes also to preaching? He greatly desired to know the will of God concerning this question. Because of his holy humility, he did not want to trust himself or his own prayers for an answer, so he decided to seek the divine will through the prayers of others.

He called Brother Masseo to him and said, "Go to Sister Clare and tell her in my name that, together with her most spiritual companions, she should devoutly pray God to show me whether it is better that I give myself to preaching or to prayer alone. Then go to Brother Sylvester and tell him to do the same." Brother Sylvester was so devout and holy that in prayer he prevailed with God and all that he asked was granted. He talked often with God. Therefore Saint Francis was greatly devoted to him.

Brother Masseo departed and, according to the request of Saint Francis, went to Saint Clare and then to Brother Sylvester. Brother Sylvester immediately started to pray, and while he was praying, he obtained the divine answer. He turned to Brother Masseo and said, "This is what God says to Brother Francis: God has not called him for himself alone, but that he may bear much fruit of souls, and that many through him may be saved." When he heard that, Brother Masseo returned to Saint Clare, to know what answer she had received from God. She replied that she and the other companions had the same answer from God as the one that Brother Sylvester received. Brother Masseo returned to Saint Francis, who welcomed him with much love, washing his feet and setting food before him. When he had eaten, Saint Francis called Masseo into the woods. There Saint Francis kneeled down before him and drew back his cowl. Making a cross of his arms, he asked, "What does my Lord Jesus Christ bid me do?" Brother Masseo answered, "To Brother Sylvester as to Sister Clare and to her companions, Christ revealed that his will is for you to go through the world and preach, because he has chosen you not for yourself alone but also for the salvation of others."

Then Saint Francis rose up with great fervor and said, "Let us go in the name of God." He took as his companions Brother Masseo and Brother Agnolo, holy men. Going impetuously, with no thought of way or path, they came to a walled place called Savurniano, where Saint Francis began to preach. But first he asked the swallows that were twittering to keep silence until he finished preaching, and the swallows obeyed him. He preached so fervently that for devotion all the men and women were ready to follow him and abandon the town. But Saint Francis did not let them, saying, "Do not be too hasty to depart. I will tell you what you should do for the salvation of your souls." Then he decided to begin the Third Order for the universal salvation of all people.

Leaving them comforted, with their minds turned to repentance, Saint Francis traveled on, full of fervor. He looked up and saw some trees near the road, on which were perched an almost infinite number of birds. He marveled at the sight and said to his companions, "Wait for me here on the road, and I will go and preach to the birds my sisters." He went into the field and began to preach to the birds on the ground. Soon those in the trees came to him, and all of them stood still together until he finished preaching. Even then they did not leave until he gave them his blessing. As Brother Masseo later told Brother James of Massa, when Saint Francis went among them touching them with his robe, none of them moved.

This is what Saint Francis preached: "My sisters the birds, you are greatly indebted to God your Creator, and always and in every place you should praise God for giving you liberty to fly wherever you want, and clothing you with double and triple clothing. Moreover, God preserved your seed in Noah's ark so that your race might not be destroyed. Again, you are in God's debt for the element of the air that God has appointed for you. Furthermore, you *neither sow nor reap and yet* God *feeds* you and gives you rivers and fountains to drink from. God gives you mountains and valleys for your refuge, and high trees to build your nests. Since you do not know how to sew or spin, God clothes you and your little ones. Your Creator must love you since God gives you so many benefits. Guard yourselves, therefore, my sisters the birds, from the sin of ingratitude, and always remember to give praise to God."

When Saint Francis spoke these words, all the birds opened their beaks and stretched out their necks, spread their wings, reverently bowed their heads to the ground and showed by their motions and their songs that the holy father delighted them. Saint Francis rejoiced with them and marveled at such a multitude of birds and their most beautiful diversity and their attention and fearlessness. Therefore he devoutly praised the Creator in them. Finally, when he had finished preaching, Saint Francis made the sign of the cross over them and dismissed them.

Then all those birds rose into the air with wonderful songs. According to the form of the cross that Saint Francis had made over them, they divided themselves into four bands; and one flew toward each of the four quarters of the world. So the preaching of the cross of Christ, renewed by Saint Francis, was about to be carried through all the world by him and by his brothers, who, like the birds, possess nothing of their own in this world but commit their lives wholly to the providence of God.

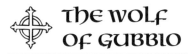

THE WOLF OF GUBBIO

From *The Little Flowers of Saint Francis*, Chapter 21

This story of how Francis made peace between a town and a rampaging wolf seems more fairy tale than history. Some modern retellings have made the wolf a bandit chief. But there are shrines in Gubbio for both the wolf's cave and his grave.

While Saint Francis lived in the city of Gubbio, there appeared in the surrounding area a ferocious wolf, which devoured not only animals but also men and women. All the citizens were afraid because he often came near the city, and all men went armed when they left the city, as if they were going to battle. Still anyone who happened to encounter the wolf alone was not able to defend himself. For dread of this wolf things got so bad that no one dared to leave the city.

Saint Francis, having compassion on the people of the city, decided to meet this wolf, although the citizens warned him not to do so. Making the sign of the cross, he went from the city with his companions, putting all his trust in God. Because the others were afraid to go farther, Saint Francis alone took the road toward the wolf's territory. While many citizens who had come out to watch this miracle were looking on, the wolf charged at Saint Francis with open mouth. Saint Francis advanced toward him and, making over him the sign of the most holy cross, called the wolf to him and said, "Come here, Brother Wolf. I command you in Christ's name to do no harm to me or to any other."

O marvelous thing! Scarcely had Saint Francis made the sign of the cross than the ferocious wolf instantly closed his mouth and stopped running. In obedience to that command, he came, gentle as a lamb, and laid himself down at the feet of Saint Francis. Then Saint Francis spoke to him, "Brother Wolf, you do a lot of damage in these parts, and you have committed great crimes, killing the creatures of God without God's permission. Not only have you killed and devoured beasts, but you have also had the boldness to kill people, made in the image of God. For this you deserve the gallows as a thief and most iniquitous murderer. All cry out against you and complain, and all this city is your enemy. But I desire, Brother Wolf, to make peace between you and them so that you no more offend them and that they may forgive you all your past offenses and neither men nor dogs may pursue you anymore." At those words, the wolf, by moving his body and tail and eyes, and by bowing his head, showed that he accepted what Saint Francis said and intended to comply.

Then Saint Francis spoke again, "Brother Wolf, since it seems good to you to make and keep this peace, I promise you that as long as you live, I will ask the people of this city to give you food regularly so that you will no longer be hungry. I know well that whatever evil you have done was through hunger.

But since I beg for you this gift, I ask you, Brother Wolf, to promise me that you will never again injure any human being or any animal. Do you promise me this?" And the wolf, by bowing his head, gave clear indication that he promised it.

Saint Francis continued, "Brother Wolf, I ask you to swear me fealty concerning this promise so that I may trust you completely." Then Saint Francis held forth his hand to receive his fealty, and the wolf lifted up his right forefoot and put it with friendly confidence in the hand of Saint Francis, giving thereby such token of fealty as he was able.

Saint Francis said, "Brother Wolf, I command you in the name of Jesus Christ to come now with me, doubting nothing, and let us establish this peace in the name of God." The wolf went with him obediently, like a gentle lamb.

The citizens marveled at the meeting of the two. Soon the news spread throughout the city, and all the people—men and women, great and small, young and old—thronged to the piazza to see the wolf with Saint Francis.

When all the folk were gathered together, Saint Francis began to preach to them, saying, among other things, how much the jaws of hell are to be feared when the jaws of a little beast can hold so great a multitude in fear! "Turn then, dearest ones, turn to God, and do proper penance for your sins, and God will save you from the wolf in this present world and from the fire of hell in that which is to come." And when he had finished preaching, Saint Francis said,

"Listen, brothers and sisters. Brother Wolf, who is here before you, has promised and sworn fealty to me, that he will make peace with you and never again harm you in any way. Now you must promise to give him every day what he needs. I guarantee that he will faithfully observe this covenant of peace." Then all the people with one voice promised to provide food for him continually.

Saint Francis asked the wolf before them all, "And you, Brother Wolf, do you promise to observe the covenant of peace that you have made with these people, that you will not harm human or beast or any creature?" The wolf kneeled down, bowed his head and, with gentle movements of his body and tail and ears, showed as far as he was able his determination to keep that covenant completely.

Said Saint Francis, "Brother Wolf, as you did me fealty concerning this promise outside the gate, so now I ask you to do me fealty, before all the people, concerning this promise, and that you will not deceive me concerning my promise and guarantee that I have given for you." Then the wolf, lifting up his right foot, put it in the hand of Saint Francis. All the people were filled with such great joy and wonder, because of their devotion toward the saint, the strangeness of the miracle, and the new peace with the wolf, that they began to shout to heaven. They praised and blessed God who had sent them Saint Francis, who, by his merits, had freed them from the jaws of the cruel beast.

Afterward, the wolf lived two years in Gubbio and entered familiarly into the houses, going from door to door, neither doing injury to anyone nor receiving any. The people courteously nourished him, and no dog ever barked at him. After two years, Brother Wolf died of old age. The citizens lamented his death, because as long as they saw him going so gently through their city, they could better recall the virtue and sanctity of Saint Francis.

CONVERSION THROUGH PRAYER AND EXAMPLE

From *The Mirror of Perfection*, Chapters 72 and 73

The Mirror of Perfection *seems to be based on the memories of Brother Leo together with Thomas of Celano's first* Life *and other sources, compiled in the late thirteenth century. In this selection, Francis tries to teach the Brothers that exemplary lives are more convincing than eloquent and learned words. The "Ministers" are the leaders of the order.*

The most holy father did not wish his Brothers to yearn for learning and books, but taught them to build their lives on holy humility, to practice pure simplicity and devout prayer, and to love Lady Poverty, on which the saints and first Brothers had established themselves. He used to say that this was the only sure road to their own salvation and the edification of others, because Christ, whom we are called to follow, showed and taught us the way by his teaching and example alone.

Looking into the future, the blessed father knew through the Holy Spirit, and often told the Brothers, that in the hope of edifying others, many would abandon their vocation, which is holy humility, pure simplicity, prayer and devotion, and the love of Lady Poverty. He said, "Because they will think themselves more gifted, more filled with devotion, more fired with love, and more enlightened by divine knowledge through their study of the Scriptures, they will as a result remain inwardly cold and empty. Consequently, they will be unable to return to their first vocation, because they will have wasted the time in useless and misguided study when they should have been following this vocation. I fear that even the grace that they seemed to possess will be taken away from them."

He added, "Many Brothers devote all their energy and zeal to the acquisition of learning, neglecting their holy vocation, and straying from the way of humility and holy prayer both in mind and in body. When they have preached to the people and learn that some have been helped or moved to penitence, they grow conceited and congratulate themselves as though the others' gain were their own. But they will have preached rather to their own condemnation and hurt, and they have really achieved nothing except as the instruments of those through whom God has obtained this result. For those whom they imagined they were edifying and converting through their own learning and preaching have been edified and converted by God through the prayers and tears of holy, poor, humble, and simple Brothers, although these holy men are not aware of it. For it is the will of God that they should know nothing of it, lest they become proud.

"These Brothers are my knights of the Round Table, who remain hidden in deserts and lonely places in order to devote themselves more completely to prayer and meditation, lamenting their own sins and the sins of others, living simply and behaving humbly, whose sanctity is known to God and at times to other Brothers but unknown to the world. When the angels present their souls before God, God will show them the fruit and reward of their labors, namely, the many souls that have been saved by their prayers and tears. And God will say to them, 'My dear sons, these souls have been saved by your prayers, tears, and example, and since you have been faithful over little things, I have great things to commit to your charge. Others have preached and labored with their words of wisdom and learning, but through your merits, I have brought about the fruit of salvation. So receive the reward of your labors and the fruit of your merits, which is an everlasting kingdom gained by your humility and simplicity, and by the power of your prayers and tears.' And bearing their sheaves with them, that is, the fruit and merit of their holy humility and simplicity, these holy Brothers will enter the joy of the Lord with exultation.

"But those who have cared for nothing except to know and point out the way of salvation to others, and have made no effort to follow it themselves, will stand naked and empty-handed before the judgment seat of Christ, bearing only the sheaves of confusion, shame, and grief. Then shall the truth of holy humility and simplicity, of holy prayer and poverty, which is our vocation, be exalted, glorified, and proclaimed; the truth that those who were swollen with the wind of their learning betrayed by their own lives and by the words of their empty learning, saying that truth was falsehood, and blindly and cruelly persecuting people who walked in the truth. In that day the error and falsity of the opinions in which they lived — which they proclaimed as truth, and by which they have thrust many people into a pit of darkness — will finally be exposed in confusion, shame, and grief. And they, with their misguided opinions, will be cast into outer darkness with the spirits of darkness."

Francis, the faithful servant and perfect imitator of Christ, feeling himself wholly united to Christ through the virtue of holy humility, desired this humility in the Brothers before all other virtues. And so that they might love, desire, acquire, and preserve it, he gave them constant encouragement by his example and teaching, and particularly impressed this on the Ministers and preachers, urging them to undertake humble tasks.

He used to say that they must not allow the duties of high office or the responsibility of preaching to stand in the way of holy and devout prayer, going out for alms, doing manual labor when required, and carrying out other humble duties like the rest of the Brothers, as a good example and for the good of their own and others' souls. He said, "The Brothers under obedience are much edified when their Ministers and preachers gladly devote their time to prayer and apply themselves to humble and undistinguished tasks. Unless they do these things they cannot admonish other Brothers without embarrassment, injustice, and self-condemnation; for if we follow Christ's example, we must act rather than teach, and our acting and teaching must go together."

LETTER TO A MINISTER

This short letter, written to a Minister of the order, describes how to deal with sinners. It may have been written to Brother Elias, who was Minister General from 1221, in preparation for the Pentecost Chapter of 1223. At that meeting the Brothers revised the simple Rule that Francis had written in 1221 in preparation to submit it for the approval of Pope Honorius III.

To Brother N., Minister,

The Lord bless you. I speak to you as I am able concerning the condition of your soul. If there are persons, whether Brothers or not, who are a hindrance to you in loving the Lord God—even though some were to beat you with whips—yet you should count all these trials as favors. You should think this way and no other. Let this be like a command to you from the Lord and from me, for I know certainly that this is true obedience. Love those who do such things to you, and do not ask anything else from them except what has been granted to you. So should you love them, not wishing that they would be better Christians. And let this be more valuable to you than the peace of a hermitage.

In this way I will know that you love God and me, God's servant and yours: that there is no brother in all the world, no matter how deeply he sins, who leaves your presence without your mercy, if he wants mercy. And if he does not seek mercy, then you ask him whether he wants it. Even if he appears before you a thousand times, love him more than you love me, so you may draw him to love God. And have pity on all who are like him.

And you should tell this to the guardians when you have opportunity: that you are determined to act in this way.

Now out of all the articles in the Rule on mortal sins, let us, at the Pentecost Chapter, God helping, and with the counsel of the Brothers, make one to this effect:

If any Brother, instigated by the enemy, falls into mortal sin, let him be bound by obedience to hurry to his guardian. Let none of the Brothers who know that he has sinned cause him shame or reproach him. Rather let them have great pity on him, and keep very secret that sin of their Brother. For *those who are well have no need of a physician, but those who are sick.* Also let them be bound by obedience to send him to his guardian with a companion. Then let the guardian look on him with mercy, as he would wish another to look on him, if he were in a similar situation. If he should fall into another venial sin, let him confess to a brother who is a priest. If no priest is there, let him confess to his brother until he finds a priest who shall absolve him canonically, as it is explained in the Rule. And let them have no power of ordering any other penance beyond saying, "Go your way, and from now on do not sin again."

Hold on to this writing until Pentecost, that it may be better observed. You will be there with your Brothers, and you will arrange to have put in these things and others that are lacking in the Rule.

PARAPHRASE OF THE LORD'S PRAYER

Francis wrote this paraphrase for the use of his followers in both communal and private prayer. The text of the Lord's Prayer follows the ecumenical version for use in worship.

Our Father, most holy, Creator, Redeemer, Savior, Comforter,

in heaven, in the angels and saints enlightening them to knowledge of you, for you, Lord, are Light; inflaming them to love of you, for you, Lord, are Love; dwelling in them and filling them with blessing, for you, Lord, are the highest good, the eternal good, from whom all good proceeds, without whom nothing is good.

Hallowed be your name, may it be glorified in us by knowledge of you, that we may perceive the wideness of your blessings, the extent of your promises, the height of your majesty, the depth of your judgments.

Your kingdom come, that you may reign in us by your grace and bring us to your kingdom, where the vision of you is revealed, and your love made perfect, that we may enter your blessed presence, and enjoy you forever.

Your will be done, on earth as in heaven, that we may love you with all our hearts, ever thinking of you, and desiring you with all our souls and with all our minds; directing all our intentions to you and seeking your honor in all things; with all our strength devoting every power and faculty of mind and body to the service of your love and to no other end.

May we also love our neighbors as ourselves, drawing them to love of you with all our power; delighting in the good of others as in our own, sharing in their troubles, and giving no offense to any.

Give us today our daily bread, which is your beloved Son, Jesus Christ our Lord, in the remembrance, understanding, and reverence of the love that he bore us, and for the things that he said, did, and endured for our sakes.

Forgive us our sins through your infinite mercy and by virtue of the passion of your beloved Son, our Lord Jesus Christ, and through the merits and prayers of the most blessed Virgin Mary and of all your elect.

As we forgive those who sin against us, and since we do not forgive fully, Lord, enable us to forgive fully so that we may truly love our enemies for your sake and pray for them devoutly to you, not returning evil for evil but seeking to serve all people in you.

Save us from the time of trial, hidden or open, sudden or persistent.

And deliver us from evil, past, present, and to come.

Amen.

ADMONITIONS ON HUMILITY AND LOVE

From "The Admonitions of Francis"

"The Admonitions" is a collection of short sayings on a variety of subjects pertaining to the Christian life. According to Thomas of Celano, they were spoken to the Brothers at various times and written down at Francis's command. Although the admonitions were directed specifically to the Brothers and reflect their situation, the advice is good for all Christians.

The Lord said to Adam, "You may freely eat of every tree of the garden; but of the tree of the knowledge of good and evil you shall not eat, for in the day that you eat of it you shall die." So Adam was permitted to eat of every tree in the garden, and as long as he did not disobey, he did not sin. For people eat of the tree of the knowledge of good when they direct their will to their own ends and boast about the good that God works through them. By this means, through the instigation of the devil and their own disobedience to the command of God, the good fruit is transformed into the fruit of the knowledge of evil, and for this they have to suffer the penalty.

Our Lord says in the Gospels: "None of you can become my disciple if you do not give up all your possessions," and "Those who want to save their life will lose it." The man who renounces all his possessions and loses himself body and soul is the man who surrenders himself to obedience in the hands of his superior. Therefore, provided that it is good and is not contrary to the will of his superior, all that he does or says is true obedience. And if, while thus under obedience, he should see things that seem better and more profitable to his soul than those commanded by his superior, let him surrender his will to God in sacrifice and take care to carry out the orders of his superior. For this is true and loving obedience, acceptable to God and one's neighbor.

Should a superior give an order that is against the conscience of a subject, he is not obliged to obey, but he may not leave his superior. If his refusal brings persecution on him, he must love his persecutors all the more for God's sake. For one who would suffer persecution rather than separate himself from his brothers is living in true and perfect obedience, because one *lays down one's life for one's friends*. But there are many religious who, claiming to see a better course of action than that ordered by their superiors, look back and *return to the vomit* of their self-will. Such men are guilty of manslaughter because their evil example causes the loss of many souls.

"I came not to be served but to serve," says the Lord. Those who are appointed to rule over others may not boast of their position any more than if they were to be assigned to the duty of washing their brothers' feet. And if they are more disturbed about the possibility of losing their position than they would be about losing the duty of foot-washing, they will expose their souls to great danger.

My brothers, let us think of the Good Shepherd, who endured the Passion and Cross in order to save his sheep. Our Lord's sheep have followed him in trouble, persecution and disgrace, in hunger and thirst, in temptation and other hardships, and by so doing have received everlasting life from their Lord. It therefore brings much disgrace on us servants of God that the saints have done great things while we hope to win honor and fame merely by talking and preaching about them.

The apostle Paul tells us, "The letter kills, but the Spirit gives life." Those killed by the letter are those who want to know the words of Christ only to appear wiser and more learned than others and to amass a great fortune to bestow on their families and friends. Even religious are killed by the letter if they are not prepared to follow the spirit of the word of God, but are content merely to know it and explain it to others. But those who receive life from the spirit of the word of God are those who do not take every word that they study in its literal sense, but by their own word and example ascribe it to God most high, the Source of all good.

The Apostle Paul declares, "No one can say 'Jesus is Lord' except by the Holy Spirit," and, "There is no one who shows kindness." So whoever envies his brother because of the good that the Lord says or does through him is close to committing the sin of blasphemy, for his envy is against God most high, who is the Source and Author of all good.

Our Lord says in the Gospel, "Love your enemies." One who truly loves his enemy does not bear malice for any injury that he has received from him. Because he loves God, he grieves for the sin on the other's soul and shows his love by his actions.

Many people always blame an enemy or a neighbor whenever they themselves do wrong or suffer some hurt. This is not just, for everyone has his enemy in his own power, that is, his own body, by which he sins. Blessed is the servant who keeps such an enemy constantly under his control and wisely guards against him. For so long as he does this, no other enemy, visible or invisible, can harm him.

A servant of God may recognize whether he has the Spirit of God in this way: if when God performs any good through him his natural feelings are not puffed up—for the flesh is always the enemy of all good—and if he always remembers his own unworthiness and regards himself as the least of all.

A servant of God cannot know the extent of his patience and humility as long as all goes well with him. But when a time comes that those who should treat him well do the opposite, then he shows the true extent of his patience and humility and no more.

 # BEATITUDES

From "The Admonitions of Francis"

These sayings, generally in the form of beatitudes and often echoing the beatitudes of Christ from the Sermon on the Mount, conclude "The Admonitions," which Francis addressed to the Brothers of the order.

Blessed are the poor in spirit, for theirs is the kingdom of heaven. There are many who are regular in saying their prayers and offices, and who discipline their bodies by fasts and austere measures. But if a single word is uttered that offends them, or if they are deprived of anything, they are immediately provoked and offended. People of this sort are not poor in spirit, for one who is truly poor in spirit despises himself and shows charity towards those who strike him in the face.

Blessed are the peacemakers, for they will be called children of God. True lovers of peace are those who, in all their sufferings upon earth, remain at peace in mind and body for the love of Jesus Christ.

Blessed are the pure in heart, for they will see God. The pure in heart are those who despise earthly things and aspire to heavenly ones. They never cease to adore and see the Lord God, the living and the true, with a pure heart and soul.

Blessed is the servant who does not take greater pleasure in the good that God says or does through him than what God accomplishes through others. When anyone wants to receive more from his neighbor than he is prepared to give to the Lord his God, he is guilty of sin.

Blessed is the one who helps his neighbor in trouble, just as he would wish to be helped in similar circumstances.

Blessed is the servant who regards all that he has as belonging to God; for whoever retains anything for his own use hides his master's money; and even what he seems to have will be taken away.

Blessed is the servant who does not esteem himself better when he is praised and promoted by people than when they look on him as vile, stupid, and contemptible, for whatever a man is in the sight of God, that he is and no more. Woe to the Religious who is raised to high office by his fellows, but refuses to relinquish it. And blessed is the servant who is promoted by no desire of his own and always desires to remain at the feet of others.

Blessed is the brother whose sole joy and delight are in the most holy words and works of God, so that he leads others to the love of God with joy and gladness. And woe to the brother who loves idle and foolish chatter, and thus leads others to laughter.

Blessed is the servant who does not speak in the hope of gain, does not discuss all his affairs, and is not eager to talk, but wisely weighs his words and replies. Woe to the Religious who does not hide the favors that God has shown him within his heart, and who does not show proof of them in his behavior, but wants to tell everyone about them in hope of some gain. In so doing he has received his reward, and those who listen to him reap little benefit.

Blessed is the servant who accepts instruction, accusation, and reproof from another as patiently as he would from himself. Blessed is the servant who accepts rebuke with courtesy, obeys respectfully, confesses humbly, and makes amends gladly. Blessed is the servant who is not in a hurry to excuse himself, but humbly accepts shame and reproach for a fault even when he is not to blame.

Blessed is the one who is as humble among his subjects as among his superiors. Blessed is the servant who is always amenable to the rod of correction. The *faithful and wise servant* is one who does immediate penance for his misdeeds, both inwardly by contrition and outwardly by confession and active reparation.

Blessed is the one who loves his brother as much when he is ill and unable to help him as when he is well and able to offer help.

Blessed is the one who loves and respects his brother when he is absent as when he is present, and never says anything behind his back that he could not in love say to his face.

Blessed is the servant who is loyal to the clergy who live good lives and observe the laws of the holy Roman Church. And woe to those who despise them, for even when clergy are sinners, no one should judge them, since God alone reserves the right to judge. For since their office is concerned with the most holy body and blood of our Lord Jesus Christ, which they receive and they alone may administer to others, it is higher than all others, so that any offense against them is more serious than those committed against others in this world.

Where there is love and wisdom, there is neither fear nor ignorance.

Where there is patience and humility, there is neither anger nor vexation.

Where there is poverty with joy, there is neither greed nor avarice.

Where there is peace and meditation, there is neither anxiety nor doubt.

Where the fear of the Lord stands guard, there the enemy finds no entry.

Where there is mercy and moderation, there is neither indulgence nor harshness.

Blessed is the servant who *stores up* the favors that God has shown him as *treasures in heaven* and has no wish to disclose them to others in the hope of some advantage, for the Most High will reveal divine workings to whomever the Most High pleases. Blessed is the servant who keeps the secrets of the Lord locked away in the heart.

TESTAMENT
OF FRANCIS

Francis dictated his "Testament" in October 1226, shortly before his death. In it he offers both testimony about his own experience and advice to the members of his order.

This is how the Lord gave grace to me, Brother Francis, to begin to do penance. When I was still in sin, it seemed a very bitter thing to me to look upon people with leprosy. But the Lord brought me among them, and I lived with them a while. When I left them, what had seemed to me bitter was turned to sweetness in my soul and body. After that I lived little in the world. I left it behind me. The Lord gave me such faith in his churches that I would pray there simply, saying, "We adore you, most holy Lord Jesus Christ, here and in all your churches throughout the world. And we bless you, for by your holy cross you have redeemed the world."

Moreover, the Lord gave me—and still gives—such faith in priests who live according to the form of the holy Roman Church, by reason of their ordination, that were they to persecute me, I would still go to them. If I had all the wisdom of Solomon, I would not preach in the churches belonging to the humblest secular priests without their permission. I will do reverence to them as to all the others, and love and honor them as my lords. Nor will I consider their sins; for I discern the Son of God in them, and they are my lords. And this I do because with my bodily eyes I see nothing else in this world of the most high Son of God except his most holy body which they receive and which they alone administer to others. These most holy mysteries I will honor and venerate above all else and keep them in sacred places. When I find the most holy names of the Lord or the Lord's written words in unholy places, I will take them away and house them properly and beg others to do the same. We should also honor and revere all theologians and those who speak the most holy words of God, for they administer unto us the spirit and the life.

After the Lord had given me the care of the Brothers, no one showed me what I should do. The Most High revealed to me that I should live according to the pattern of the holy gospel. I wrote my Rule simply and in few words, and the pope confirmed it. Those who came to take up this life gave all that they had to the poor. They were content with one tunic, patched inside and out, with a cord and undershorts. We had no wish for anything else. The clergy said the office like other clergy, and the laity said the Lord's Prayer. We willingly lived in poor little deserted churches. We were simple and the servants of all. I worked with my hands, and I still will work. My strong desire is that all the other Brothers carry on some honest trade. Let those who know none learn one, not out of greed for wages, but for a good example and the prevention of idleness. When we are given no wages for our labor, let us go to the table of the Lord, begging alms from door to door. The Lord revealed to me the salutation we should offer: "God give you peace!"

Let the Brothers beware of receiving churches and dwelling places and anything else that may be built for them, except in accordance with holy poverty, to which we are vowed by the Rule. Wherever they dwell, let it be as strangers and pilgrims.

I strictly command by obedience all the Brothers throughout the world, wherever they may be, never to dare ask for any privilege from the Roman Curia, neither personally nor through anyone else—whether for a church or any other place, or under the pretext of obtaining authority to preach, or on account of persecution of the body. If they are not received in one place, let them depart into another and there do penance with the blessing of God.

I will strictly obey the Minister General of this brotherhood and any guardian whom it may please him to give me. I would be captive in his hands that I might go nowhere and do nothing except in obedience to his will—for he is my lord. Though I am a simple man and frail, yet I always want a cleric to say to me the office, as the Rule ordains. And let all the other Brothers be strictly bound to obey their guardians and to recite the office, according to the Rule. And if anyone is found who does not say the office according to the Rule or who wishes to make any change or who is not a Catholic, let all the brothers, wherever they are, be bound by obedience to bring him to the nearest custodian. And let the custodian be strictly bound by obedience to keep him fast, as a man in bonds, night and day, so that he may not escape from their hands until he be bodily given into the hands of his minister. And let the minister be strictly bound by obedience to send him by Brothers, who shall guard him night and day, as a man in bonds, until he is brought before the bishop of Ostia, who is the lord, the protector, and the corrector of this brotherhood.

And let not the Brothers say, "This is a new Rule." For this is but a remembrance, an admonition, an exhortation, and my Testament, which I, your little brother Francis, write for you, my blessed Brothers, so that we may as better Catholics observe the Rule that we have vowed to the Lord.

Let the Minister General and all the other ministers and custodians be bound by obedience neither to add to, nor to take away from these words. And let them keep this writing by them along with the Rule. And in all the chapters that they hold, when they read the Rule, read these words also. I order strictly all my Brothers, both clerics and laymen, that they add no notes to the Rule, or these words, saying, "This is how they should be understood." As the Lord enabled me to write the Rule and these words simply and clearly, so let them be understood simply, clearly, and without annotation. Observe them in holy works to the end.

May whoever observes these things be filled in heaven with the blessing of the Most High, and on earth with the blessing of God's beloved Son and the Holy Spirit the Comforter and with the virtues of heaven and all the saints. And I, little brother Francis, your servant in the Lord, confirm to you so far as I can, both within and without, this most holy blessing. Amen.

# SONG OF THE CREATURES

Francis wrote the "Song of the Creatures" in three stages.
The first part (through Mother Earth) was written in 1225.
While trying to resolve a conflict in Assisi a year later, he
wrote the verses about forgiveness and peace. The last verse,
about Sister Death, was written during his final illness.

Most High, almighty, and good Lord, yours are the praise and glory, the honor and every blessing! To you alone, Most High, are they due; and no one is worthy to name you.

Praise to you, Lord, with all your creatures; and above all to Brother Sun, who makes the day that lightens us. He is fair and shines with a great splendor. Most High, he bears your mark.

Praise to you, Lord, for Sister Moon and for the Stars. In the heavens you have framed them, clear and precious and fair.

Praise to you, Lord, for Brother Wind, for the air and the cloud, for calm and all weather by which you give sustenance to your creatures.

Praise to you, Lord, for Sister Water. Very useful is she and humble and precious and chaste.

Praise to you, Lord, for Brother Fire by whom the night is lightened. He is lovely and limber and lusty and strong.

Praise to you, Lord, for our sister, Mother Earth, who upholds and cares for us, who brings forth the many kinds of fruit, the painted flowers, and the grass.

Praise to you, Lord, for those who forgive for love of you and bear weakness and tribulations.

Blessed are those who endure in peace, for they shall be crowned by you, Most High.

Praise to you, Lord, for our sister, the Death of the Body. No one living may escape from her. Woe to those who die in mortal sin! Blessed are those who find themselves in your most holy will, for the second death cannot harm them.

Praise and bless the Lord, and give God thanks, and serve God with great humility.

CLARE FOLLOWS FRANCIS

From *The Life of Saint Clare*, Chapters 3 to 5

Clare's biography was written within a few years of her death in 1253. Thomas of Celano has been suggested as the author, though that is not certain. The author made extensive use of interviews with Clare's companions, which occurred during the process of her canonization. This selection tells her story from the time she first met with Francis until he placed her with the Benedictine Sisters at San Paolo a few miles from Assisi. In 1212, when these events took place, Palm Sunday was on March 18. Clare was eighteen.

When she heard of the now famous name of Francis who, like a new man, had restored by new virtues the path of perfection forgotten in the world, Clare at once desired to hear and see him. She was moved to this action by *the Father of spirits*, whose first prompting both had followed, though in different ways. Francis, struck by the good reputation of so favored a maiden, was no less eager to see her and converse with her. Being wholly eager for spoils and having come to depopulate the kingdom of this world, he hoped somehow to snatch this noble prey from the wicked world and restore her to her God.

Francis visited Clare, and she more often visited him, so ordering the times of their visits that their holy meetings might neither become known by others nor defamed by public gossip. Accompanied by a single confidential companion, the young woman frequently visited the man of God, leaving her father's home in secret. To her his words seemed a flame and his deeds more than human. Father Francis urged her to have contempt for the world, showing her in vivid words the barrenness of earthly hopes and the deceitfulness of earthly beauty. He poured into her ears the sweet marriage with Christ, persuading her to conserve the pearl of her virginal purity for that Blessed Spouse who out of love became man.

But why multiply words? At the request of the most holy father, who acted as smoothly as a most faithful matchmaker, the virgin did not delay in giving her consent. At once she glimpsed the heavenly joys, the sight of which made the world itself seem of small price, the desire of which made her melt away, and the love of which made her aspire after the heavenly marriage. Glowing with celestial fire, Clare looked down on the glory of earthly vanity so much that nothing of the world's applause held her affections. Dreading, moreover, the allurements of the flesh, she resolved to keep herself undefiled, desiring to make her body a temple to God alone and striving by virtue to merit marriage with the great King. Clare committed herself completely to the guidance of Francis, considering him to be, after God, the director of her steps. From that time her soul depended upon his holy admonitions, and she received with a ready heart whatever he said to her of the good Jesus. She was already weary of the beauty of worldly apparel,

and she *regarded as rubbish all the things* the world
esteems, *that she might gain Christ.*

Furthermore, so that worldly dust would not in
the future stain the unspotted mirror of her soul or
worldly contagion corrupt Clare at such a susceptible
age, the good father hurried to lead her out of the
dark world. The solemnity of Palm Sunday was
approaching when the young woman fervently went
to the man of God for counsel about her retreat from
the world—what was to be done and how she was to
do it. Father Francis told her that on the feast day
Clare, dressed in her finest, should come to the blessing of the palms with the rest of the people. On the
following night she should *go outside the camp* and her
laughter be turned into mourning for the Lord's passion.
When Sunday arrived, the young woman, radiant in
festive array among the crowd of women, entered the
church with the others.

There a noteworthy omen occurred, for whereas
the rest pressed forward to receive the branches,
Clare through modesty remained in her place without moving. Then the bishop, descending from the
steps, came to her and put a palm in her hands. The
following night Clare set about the accomplishment
of the saint's command. With some trusted companions, she began her longed-for flight. But not wishing
to leave by the usual door, she, with a strength that
astonished herself, broke open another one that was
walled up by beams and stones. Thus leaving behind
her home, city, and kindred, Clare hastened to Saint
Mary of the Portiuncula.

The Brothers who were keeping vigil at the little altar with lighted torches received the virgin Clare. Immediately casting aside the filth of Babylon, she there gave a bill of divorce to the world and forsook her various ornaments, her hair being cut by the Brothers. It would not be proper that the order of virginity beginning here should flower elsewhere than in the sanctuary of her who, first and most worthy of all, was alone a virgin and a mother. This is also where the new army of the poor under the leadership of Francis took on its happy beginnings, so that it might be clear that both orders were brought forth by the Mother of Mercies in her inn. But after Clare had received the holy garments of penance before the altar of the blessed Mary, and after the humble handmaid had been married to Christ as if by the throne of this virgin, Saint Francis immediately led her to the Church of San Paolo, to stay there until the Most High should provide another place.

When the news reached her heartbroken relatives, they condemned Clare's action and plans. Banding together, they hurried to the place and tried to obtain what they could not. They tried force, dire warnings, and empty promises, urging Clare to withdraw from such a sorry plight, which was unworthy of her birth and unheard of in those parts. But Clare took hold of the altar cloths and bared her tonsured head. She declared that nothing would separate her from the service of Christ. Her courage increased as the war waged by her relatives grew stronger. Love wounded by ill treatment gave her strength. For many days she endured this obstacle in the way of the Lord. While her relatives set themselves against her holy plan, Clare's courage did not fail nor did her fervor diminish. Between harsh words and deeds, she encouraged herself to hope. Finally her relatives, withdrawing their opposition, quieted down.

# ḣumility aṅd poverty

From *The Life of Saint Clare*, Chapters 8 and 9

This selection from Clare's biography contains examples of her humility and her devotion to poverty. The "serving Sisters" are those who worked outside the convent in hospitals or at other tasks.

Clare, the cornerstone and noble foundation of her order, sought from the very first to raise the edifice of all virtues upon the basis of holy humility. She promised holy obedience to the blessed Francis, and she never turned back from this promise. During the three years that followed her conversion, Clare declined the name and office of abbess, humbly wishing to be subject rather than to be set over others, and to serve most willingly among the daughters of Christ rather than to be served. But at the Blessed Francis's urging, she finally undertook the government of the Ladies.

Because of assuming this office, fear and not haughtiness arose in her heart; her freedom was diminished rather than increased. The more she was seen to be raised above others by any kind of governance, the more lowly, the more fit to serve, and the less worthy of esteem she was in her own eyes. She never shrank from any menial duty. She often poured water on the hands of the Sisters, assisted those who were infirm and served those who were eating. It was with great reluctance that she ever commanded anything. She preferred to perform a task herself than to impose it on the Sisters. With her noble spirit, Clare waited upon the Sisters who were ill and washed them, neither shirking what was disagreeable nor dreading what was disgusting. She often washed the feet of the serving Sisters returning from outside, and having washed their feet, she would bend to kiss them. She was once washing the feet of a certain serving Sister and, being about to kiss them, the serving Sister, not tolerating such great humility, withdrew her foot, thus striking her lady in the face. But Clare, gently grasping the serving Sister's foot again, imprinted a fervent kiss upon its sole.

Her poverty in regard to all things included the poverty of spirit that is true humility. In the very beginning of her conversion, Clare sold the inheritance from her father and, keeping none of the money for herself, gave it all to the poor. Thus, having left the outside world and being enriched inside, she was able, not being burdened with a purse, to run after Christ. The pact that she made with holy poverty was so strict and she gained such a love for it that she wanted to have nothing but the Lord Christ, nor did she permit her daughters to possess anything else. For she knew that the *one pearl of great value*, the heavenly desire that she had bought by *selling all that she had*, was not to be possessed along with a gnawing desire for worldly things. She frequently told the Sisters that the community would be pleasing to God only when it was rich in poverty, and that it could remain firm forever only if it was always fortified by the most exalted poverty.

She encouraged them to be conformed in the little nest of poverty to Christ the Poor One, whom his poor little mother laid as a baby in a narrow manger. With this special reminder Clare adorned her breast, as if with a golden necklace, so that the dust of worldly things would not creep into her heart. Wishing that her order should bear the title of poverty, Clare petitioned Innocent III, of happy memory, for the privilege of poverty. This magnificent man, congratulating Clare upon such fervor, declared hers to be a unique proposal, since never before had such privilege been demanded of the Apostolic See. And so that an unusual favor might respond to an unusual request, the pontiff, with great joy, wrote the first letters of the requested privilege with his own hand. Pope Gregory, of happy memory, a man most worthy of the chair as he was most venerable in merits, loved the saint dearly with a paternal affection. When he was seeking to persuade her that, because of the condition of the times and the dangers of the age, she should consent to have some possessions he generously offered, she resisted with an unyielding resolve and would in no way acquiesce. To this, the pontiff answered: "If you fear your vow, we release you from the vow." "Holy Father," she said, "never do I wish to be released in any way from following Christ forever."

She gladly received the fragments of bread and other odds and ends that Brothers brought from what they had begged, and as if saddened by whole loaves, she rejoiced in the broken pieces. In short, she tried to conform by a most perfect poverty to the poor Crucified One, to the end that no perishable thing might separate the Lover from his beloved or hinder her course toward God.

# SECOND LETTER TO AGNES OF PRAGUE

Agnes of Prague (1203–82) was the daughter of King Ottakar of Bohemia and Queen Constance of Hungary. After rejecting marriage proposals from Emperor Frederick II, she moved into a Franciscan monastery that she had built, intent on imitating the life of Clare and the Poor Ladies at San Damiano. Clare wrote four (surviving) letters of encouragement to Agnes. This second letter was written about 1235, a year or more after Agnes began her religious life.

To the daughter of the *King of kings*, the servant of the *Lord of lords*, the most worthy spouse of Jesus Christ, and therefore the most noble queen, Lady Agnes: from Clare, the *worthless slave* of the Poor Ladies, greetings and a wish for your perseverance in a life of the highest poverty.

I give thanks to the Giver of grace from whom, we believe, *every generous* and *perfect gift* proceeds because God has adorned you with such splendors of virtue and given you such marks of perfection that, since you have become such a diligent imitator of the Father of all perfection, God's eyes do not see any imperfection in you.

This is the perfection that will prompt the King to take you himself in the heavenly bridal chamber where the King is seated in glory on a starry throne because you have despised the splendors of an earthly kingdom and considered of little value the offers of an imperial marriage. Instead, as someone zealous for the holiest poverty, in the spirit of great humility and the most ardent love you have *followed in the steps* of Christ to whom you have become worthy to be joined as a spouse.

But since I know that you are adorned with many virtues, I will spare my words and not weary you with needless speech, even though nothing seems superfluous to you if you can draw from it some consolation. Because *there is need of only one thing*, I bear witness to that one thing and encourage you, for love of the one to whom you have offered yourself as a *sacrifice, holy and acceptable*, that, like another Rachel, you always remember your resolution and be conscious of how you began.

What you hold, may you always hold. What you do, may you always do and never abandon. But with swift pace, light step, and unswerving feet, so that even your steps stir up no dust, go forward securely, joyfully, and swiftly on the path of prudent happiness. May you believe nothing, agree with nothing, that would dissuade you from this resolution or that would *put a stumbling block* for you *in the way*, so that *you may offer your vows to the Most High* in the pursuit of the perfection to which the Spirit of the Lord has called you.

In all of this, follow the counsel of our venerable father, our Brother Elias, the Minister General, so that you may walk more securely in *the way of* the *commandments* of the Lord. Prize it beyond the advice of the others and cherish it as dearer to you than any gift. If anyone would tell you something else or suggest something that would hinder your perfection or seem contrary to your divine vocation, even though you must respect him, do not follow his counsel. As a poor virgin, embrace the poor Christ.

Look upon him who became contemptible for you, and follow him, making yourself contemptible in the world for him. Your Spouse, though *the most handsome of men*, became, for your salvation, the lowest of men, despised, struck, scourged untold times, and then died amid the sufferings of the cross. O most noble Queen, gaze upon him, consider him, contemplate him, as you desire to imitate him.

If you suffer with him, you *will reign with him*; if you weep with him, you shall rejoice with him; if you die with him on the cross of tribulation, you shall possess heavenly mansions in the splendor of the saints, and in *the book of life*, your *name* shall be called glorious among people.

Because of this, you shall share always the glory of the kingdom of heaven in place of earthly and passing things, and everlasting treasures instead of those that perish, and you shall live forever.

Farewell, most dear sister, yes, and lady, because of the Lord, your Spouse. Commend me and my sisters to the Lord in your fervent prayers, for we rejoice in the good things of the Lord that the Lord works in you through divine grace.

Commend us truly to your sisters as well.

FOURTH LETTER TO AGNES OF PRAGUE

Clare wrote this letter to Agnes of Prague in 1253, shortly before Clare's death. In it she speaks of Christ as the "spotless mirror" in whom we see what we might be.

To her who is the half of her soul and the special shrine of her heart's deepest love, to the illustrious queen and bride of the Lamb, the eternal King: to the Lady Agnes, her most dear mother and, of all the others, her favorite daughter: from Clare, a *worthless slave* of Christ and a useless handmaid of his handmaids in the monastery of San Damiano of Assisi: health and a prayer that she may sing a new song with the other most holy *virgins before the throne* of God and of the Lamb and *follow the Lamb wherever he goes.*

O mother and daughter, spouse of the King of all ages, if I have not written to you as often as your soul and mine desire, do not wonder or think that the fire of love for you glows less sweetly in the heart of your mother. No, this is the difficulty: the lack of messengers and the obvious dangers of the roads. Now, however, as I write to your love, I rejoice and exult with you in the *joy inspired by the Holy Spirit*, O bride of Christ. Since you have totally abandoned the vanities of this world, like another most holy virgin, Saint Agnes, you have been marvelously espoused to the spotless *Lamb who takes away the sin of the world.*

Happy, indeed, is she to whom it is given to share this sacred banquet, to cling with all her heart to him whose beauty all the heavenly hosts admire unceasingly, whose love inflames our love, whose contemplation is our refreshment, whose graciousness is our joy, whose gentleness fills us to overflowing, whose remembrance brings a gentle light, whose fragrance will revive the dead, whose glorious vision will be the happiness of all the citizens of the heavenly Jerusalem.

Since this vision is *the reflection of God's glory*, the *reflection of eternal light* and the *spotless mirror*, look upon that mirror each day, O queen and spouse of Jesus Christ, and continually study your face within it so that you may adorn yourself inside and out with beautiful robes and cover yourself with the flowers and garments of all the virtues, as becomes the daughter and most chaste bride of the most high King. Indeed, blessed poverty, holy humility, and indescribable love are reflected in that mirror as, with the grace of God, you can contemplate them throughout the entire mirror.

Look first in this mirror at the poverty of him who was placed in a manger and wrapped in swaddling clothes. O marvelous humility, O astonishing poverty! The King of the angels, the Lord of heaven and earth, is laid in a manger! Then dwell on the holy humility, the blessed poverty, the untold labors and burdens that he endured for the redemption of all humanity. Finally, in this same mirror contemplate the indescribable love that led him to suffer on the wood of the cross and die there the most shameful kind of death. Therefore, that mirror, suspended on the wood of the cross, urged those who passed by to consider, saying, "All you who pass by, look and see if there is any sorrow like my sorrow!" Let us answer him with one voice and spirit, as he said, "My soul continually thinks of it and is bowed down within me!" From this moment, then, O queen of our heavenly King, let yourself be inflamed more strongly with the fervor of love!

As you contemplate further his ineffable delights, eternal riches, and honors, and sigh for them in the great desire and love of your heart, may you cry out: "Draw me after you! We will run in the fragrance of your perfumes, O heavenly Spouse! I will run and not tire, until you bring me to the banqueting house, until your left hand is under my head and your right hand will embrace me happily, and you will kiss me with the happiest kisses of your mouth."

In this contemplation, may you remember your poor little mother, knowing that I have inscribed the happy memory of you indelibly on the tablets of my heart, holding you dearer than all the others.

What more can I say? Let the tongue of the flesh be silent when I seek to express my love for you. And let the tongue of the Spirit speak, because the love that I have for you, O blessed daughter, can never be fully expressed by the tongue of the flesh, and even what I have written is an inadequate expression.

I beg you to receive my words with kindness and devotion, seeing in them at least the motherly affection that in the fire of love I feel daily toward you and your daughters, to whom I warmly commend myself and my daughters in Christ. On their part, these very daughters of mine, especially the most prudent virgin Agnes, our sister, recommend themselves in the Lord to you and your daughters.

Farewell, my dearest daughter, to you and to your daughters, until we meet at the throne *of the glory of our great God*, and desire this for us.

Inasmuch as I can, I recommend to your love the bearers of this letter, our dearly beloved Brother Amatus, *beloved by God and people*, and Brother Bonagura. Amen.

SELECTIONS FROM THE TESTAMENT OF CLARE

These selections from Clare's "Testament" include both her own testimony about the origins of her order and her hope that Sisters to come will remain true to its foundation in poverty, simplicity, humility, and the love of Christ.

Almost immediately after his conversion, while Father Francis had neither Brothers nor companions, when he was building the Church of San Damiano, he was led to abandon the world completely. Climbing the wall of that church, he shouted in French to some poor people who were standing nearby, "Come and help me build the monastery of San Damiano, because ladies will dwell here who will glorify our heavenly Father throughout the holy church by their celebrated and holy manner of life."

The most high heavenly Father saw fit in divine mercy and grace to enlighten my heart to do penance according to the example and teaching of our most blessed Father Francis, shortly after his own conversion. I, together with the few Sisters whom the Lord had given me soon after my conversion, voluntarily promised him obedience, since the Lord had given us the Light of divine grace through his holy life and teaching.

When the blessed Francis saw that, although we were physically weak and frail, we did not shirk deprivation, poverty, hard work, distress, or the shame or contempt of the world—rather, as he and his Brothers often saw for themselves, we considered all such trials as great delights after the example of the saints and their brothers—he rejoiced greatly in the Lord. And moved by compassion for us, he promised to have always, both through himself and through his order, the same loving care and special concern for us as for his own Brothers.

Thus, by the will of God and our most blessed Father Francis, we went to live at the Church of San Damiano. There, in a short time, the Lord increased our number by divine mercy and grace so that what the Lord had predicted through the saint might be fulfilled. We had stayed in another place before that, but only for a little while.

Later on our Father Francis wrote a form of life for us, indicating especially that we should persevere always in holy poverty. While he was living, he was not content to encourage us by many words and examples to love and observe holy poverty. He also gave many us writings so that after his death, we should not turn away from it. The Son of God never wished to abandon this holy poverty while he lived in the world, and our most blessed Father Francis, following his footprints, never departed, either in example or in teaching, from the holy poverty that he had chosen for himself and for the Brothers.

Therefore, I, Clare, the handmaid of Christ and of the Poor Sisters of the Monastery of San Damiano—although unworthy—and the little plant of the holy father, consider together with my sisters our most high profession and the command of so great a father. We also take note in some Sisters of the frailty that we feared in ourselves after the death of our holy Father Francis, who was our pillar of strength and, after God, our one consolation and support. Thus time and again, we bound ourselves to our Lady, most holy Poverty, so that after my death, the Sisters present and to come would never abandon her.

As I have always been most eager and careful to observe and to have the other Sisters observe the holy poverty that we have promised the Lord and our holy Father Francis, so, too, the others who will succeed me in office should be bound always to observe it and have it observed by the other sisters. For even greater security, I took care to have our profession of most holy poverty, which we promised our Father Francis, strengthened with privileges by Pope Innocent, during whose pontificate we had our beginning, and by his successors. We did this so that we would never or in any way depart from it.

The Lord gave us our most blessed Father Francis as founder, planter, and helper in the service of Christ and in the things we have promised to God and to himself as our father. While he was living he always in word and in deed cherished and took care of us, his little plant. For these reasons I commend my sisters, both those present and those to come, to the successor of our blessed Father Francis and to the entire Order, so that they may always help us to progress in serving God more perfectly and above all to observe most holy poverty in a more perfect manner.

In the Lord Jesus Christ, I urge all my Sisters, both those present and those to come, to strive always to imitate the way of holy simplicity, humility, and poverty and to preserve the integrity of our holy manner of life, as we were taught by our blessed Father Francis from the beginning of our conversion to Christ. Thus, may they always maintain a good name, both among those who are far off and those who are near, not by their own merits but solely by the mercy and grace of our Benefactor, *the Father of mercies*.

Loving one another with the love of Christ, let the love you have in your hearts be shown outwardly in your deeds so that compelled by such an example, the Sisters may always grow in love of God and in love for one another.

I also beg that the Sister who will have the office of caring for the sisters will strive to exceed others more by her virtues and holy life than by her office so that encouraged by her example, the Sisters may obey her not so much out of duty but out of love. Let her be prudent and attentive to her sisters just as a good mother is to her daughters; and especially let her provide for them according to the needs of each one from the things that the Lord shall give. Let her also be so kind and so available that all may reveal their needs with trust and have access to her at any hour with confidence as they see fit, both for her sake and that of her Sisters.

But the Sisters who are subjects should keep in mind that for the Lord's sake, they have given up their own wills. Therefore, I ask that they obey their mother as they have promised the Lord of their own free will so that seeing the charity, humility, and unity they have toward one another, their mother might more lightly bear all the burdens of her office. Thus, what is bitter might be turned into sweetness for her because of their holy way of life.

Because the way is straight and *the gate is narrow that leads to life, there are few* who walk on it and enter through it. And if there are some who walk that way for a time, there are very few who persevere in it. How blessed are those to whom it has been given to walk that way and persevere to the end!

APPENDIX

Reading Spiritual Classics for Personal and Group Formation

Many Christians today are searching for more spiritual depth, for something more than simply being good church members. That quest may send them to the spiritual practices of New Age movements or of Eastern religions such as Zen Buddhism. Christians, though, have their own long spiritual tradition, a tradition rich with wisdom, variety, and depth.

The great spiritual classics testify to that depth. They do not concern themselves with mystical flights for a spiritual elite. Rather, they contain very practical advice and insights that can support and shape the spiritual growth of any Christian. We can all benefit by sitting at the feet of the masters (both male and female) of Christian spirituality.

Reading spiritual classics is different from most of the reading we do. We have learned to read to master a text and extract information from it. We tend to read quickly, to get through a text. And we summarize as we read, seeking the main point. In reading spiritual classics, though, we allow the text to master and form us. Such formative reading goes more slowly, more reflectively, allowing time for God to speak to us through the text. God's word for us may come as easily from a minor point or even an aside as from the major point.

Formative reading requires that you approach the text in humility. Read as a seeker, not an expert. Don't demand that the text meet your expectations for what an "enlightened" author should write. Humility means accepting the author as another imperfect human, a product of his or her own time and situation. Learn to celebrate what is foundational in an author's writing without being overly disturbed by what is peculiar to the author's life and times. Trust the text as a gift from both God and the author, offered to you for your benefit—to help you grow in Christ.

To read formatively, you must also slow down. Feel free to reread a passage that seems to speak specially to you. Stop from time to time to reflect on what you have been reading. Keep a journal for these reflections. Often the act of writing can itself prompt further, deeper reflection. Keep your notebook open and your pencil in hand as you read. You might not get back to that wonderful insight later. Don't worry that you are not getting through an entire passage—or even the first paragraph! Formative reading is about depth rather than breadth, quality rather than quantity. As you read, seek God's direction for your own life. Timeless truths have their place but may not be what is most important for your own formation here and now.

As you read the passage, you might keep some of these questions running through your mind:

- How is what I'm reading true of my own life? Where does it reflect my own *experience*?

- How does this text challenge me? What new *direction* does it offer me?

- What must I change to put what I am reading into practice? How can I *incarnate* it, let this word become flesh in my life?

You might also devote special attention to sections that upset you. What is the source of the disturbance? Do you want to argue theology? Are you turned off by cultural differences? Or have you been skewered by an insight that would turn your life upside down if you took it seriously? Let your journal be a dialogue with the text.

If you find yourself moving from reading the text to chewing over its implications to praying, that's great! Spiritual reading is really the first step in an ancient way of prayer called *lectio divina* or "divine reading." Reading leads naturally into reflection on what you have read (meditation). As you reflect on what the text might mean for your life, you may well want to ask for God's help in living out any new insights or direction you have perceived (prayer). Sometimes such prayer may lead you further into silently abiding in God's presence (contemplation). And, of course, the process is only really completed when it begins to make a difference in the way we live (incarnation).

As good as it is to read spiritual classics in solitude, it is even better to join with others in a small group for mutual formation or "spiritual direction in common." This is *not* the same as a study group that talks about spiritual classics. A group for mutual formation would have similar goals as for an individual's reading: to allow the text to shine its light on the *experiences* of the group members, to suggest new *directions* for their lives and practical ways of *incarnating* these directions. Such a group might agree to focus on one short passage from a classic at each meeting (even if members have read more). Discussion usually goes much deeper if all the members have already read and reflected on the passage before the meeting and bring their journals.

Such groups need to watch for several potential problems. It is easy to go off on a tangent (especially if it takes the focus off the members' own experience and onto generalities). At such times a group leader might bring the group's attention back to the text: "What does our author say about that?" Or, "How do we experience that in our own lives?" When a group member shares a problem, others may be tempted to try to "fix" it. This is much less helpful than sharing similar experiences and how they were handled (for good or ill). "Sharing" someone else's problems (whether that person is in or out of the group) should be strongly discouraged.

One person could be designated as leader, to be responsible for opening and closing prayers; to be the first to share or respond to the text; and to keep notes during the discussion to highlight recurring themes, challenges, directives, or practical steps. These responsibilities could also be shared among several members of the group or rotated.

For further information about formative reading of spiritual classics, try *A Practical Guide to Spiritual Reading* by Susan Annette Muto. *Shaped by the Word* by Robert Mulholland (Upper Room Books) covers formative reading of the Bible. *Good Things Happen: Experiencing Community in Small Groups* by Dick Westley is an excellent resource on forming small groups of all kinds.